THE BEST BUSINESS

An Allegory of the Twelve Steps

By
A Grateful Recovering
Alcoholic

The Best Business
An Allegory on the Twelve Steps

Copyright 2009
by the Anonymous Author

Copies available directly from
www.createspace.com/**3402804**

or from
www.amazon.com

Quantity discounts available

QUOTIDIAN PUBLISHERS
377 River Road
Cushing, ME 04563
(207) 809-1167
(207) 712-9164
judydownmaine@roadrunner.com

CONTENTS

HISTORY OF EARLY BUSINESS LEADERS

In the midst of a Great Depression that few remember now, and most others would rather forget, two well-educated and proud men, both born in the tough-minded little state of Vermont, acknowledged with great sadness that their small businesses had gone belly-up. It was the year 1935 when they met in Akron, Ohio, and a painful time for both of them, because great effort had gone into the management of their corporations. Bill had spent much of his adult life in the financial sector, while Bob had dealt mostly with medical products; they were loathe to admit total defeat and to quit the businesses entirely because their products, though flawed, had some redeeming qualities. Besides, although finding some excuse would have been a relief, they knew that the state of the economy at that time was not to blame in any way. They were in deep trouble because of one reason only: the arrogant, self-willed leadership of their CEOs (Chief Executive Officers).

As the two desperate men shared corporate secrets, they became increasingly honest with each other, finally admitting to gross indiscretions, sloppy manufacturing, missed shipping dates and poor quality control. It became clear that their whole system needed to be scrapped, that a total re-tooling of their plants and practices was the only answer. And a new CEO must be hired immediately.

Over time, as they worked with other small business people, they were able to suggest twelve simple steps for redesigning the production methods of any personal business. With this background in mind, the tale of the rise and demise of Ethyl and Morph EGO is better understood.

THE BEST BUSINESS

This is how it happened.

A few years ago a young couple, caught up as they were in the excitement of operating and expanding their young business, found themselves filled with grandiose dreams of conquering the world. Their names, laughably if not surprisingly, were Hope and Hero Best, and their little enterprise (aptly titled LIFE, Inc.), was duly registered with the Secretary of State. They were intelligent, well-meaning young adults, and seriously ambitious. Their parents had painstakingly imparted everything they knew about running The Business, and the old-fashioned messages were hackneyed. The Mothers repeated various forms of the philosophy "It just isn't done, my dear," and the Fathers punctuated their explanations with "Because that's the way it's done!" The couple never admitted to their confusion.

Theirs was not a Business in the ordinary sense, but a personal enterprise, and the primary product was difficult to package and enormously valuable; it was *relationships.* No one had ever offered them a Small Business Manual; they doubted that one even existed. Oh, it's true that several institutions were available for direction -- schools, churches and governments spewing forth "you musts" and "thou shalt nots" that somehow failed to take into account the inner needs and creativity and uniqueness of these two sensitive human beings.

CEOs HIRED TO RUN THE BUSINESS

Naturally a little shy and insecure in themselves, they immediately took on a dynamic and experienced couple, Ethyl and Morph EGO, to run The Business for them. This sophisticated duo came cheap, and promised immediate and long-lasting success. Their promotional literature leaned heavily on instant gratification, computer-enhanced social skills and cosmetically heightened sexual attractiveness, without the burden of too much personal effort. It was a sales pitch the Bests found it difficult to refuse, and when Ethyl presented them with her rendition of Life's new four-color trademark -- a crystal bowl of air-brushed crimson cherries -- they were completely won over. Who could blame them? They believed the stories of the EGOs power and potential. No one ever mentioned a down side.

BUSINESS DISINTEGRATES

These CEOs became such good friends, such inseparable pals, such supporters and comforters in good times and bad, that at last the owners couldn't imagine Life without them.

Then little things began to go wrong in The Business. At first it was subtle stuff: a box of Honesty shipped out with a few defective pieces, or a bag of Courtesy returned with complaints that small chips of Anger had showed up in the mix. As the years went on, Ethyl and Morph stripped more of the decision-making power from the Bests, who were entirely willing to allow them free rein. After all, they viewed themselves as the proud owners of Life! But whenever the couple tried to make a decision from their inner spirit and integrity, the EGOs talked them out of it.

All too soon the product line was drastically restructured. Truckloads of Blame and Resentment, already dusty with Shame, rolled from the shipping bays. Little boxes of Fibs were stacked beside huge containers of Whoppers. Sometimes the production of Lies continued for weeks on end.

Eventually the EGOs introduced a new line of packaging in a muted blue and somber black with slashes of red lettering and a harsher bowl of cherries, to reflect the altered style and direction of the Business. Ethyl explained that the color scheme projected strength of purpose, but, to the discerning consumer, everything that came off the line seemed wrapped in tones of Negativity.

The EGOs had a good explanation for every obvious mistake, like the decreasing revenues, the shoddy workmanship and the dishonest advertising. They blamed the economy, the unethical tactics of other small businesses, a lack of communication ... until eventually Hope and Hero found themselves not caring much about The Business at all. Funny how their early ambition and enthusiasm had soured, turning first into apathy, then depression, and finally despair.

1. ADMISSION OF BANKRUPTCY

But the Bests were now older and less naive than they longed to appear. Their almost simultaneous flashes of insight convinced them that, yes, The Business was indeed bankrupt. Checking into back records, they discovered that it had been insolvent for many years. The Office for Customer Relations had been disbanded long ago, and every product on the Character Assembly Line was suspect. The Best Business had literally lost its reason for existing. Only a major change in leadership and direction could salvage it -- unless it were already too late.

Still in denial of the real culprits, they turned to Ethyl and Morph once again for courage, and were soothed and sweet-talked for a very long Saturday night. Sunday morning, heads pounding, Hero had a sudden flash of insight: the EGOs were the cause of this debacle, tacitly supported by their own irresponsibility. Immediately he had what could only be termed a Change of Heart.

Hope thought a good deal of it was her husband's fault, but she went along with his decisions, as she usually did. They quit trying to survive on the same old terms, and admitted sadly to each other that they'd reached some kind of financial and emotional bottom.

Hero went so far as to type up a defiant memo declaring * EGO MUST GO * in bold caps, although he was afraid to send it to the mailroom for distribution. Instead, he gave the CEOs a month off with pay, and then raged at Hope, "They've got to be fired. Permanently!"

But his wife was still hesitant, realizing that she and Hero knew very little about operating The Business of Life on their own. Morph and Ethyl had guided them by the hand too long. Who would comfort them when they hurt? Who would rescue them if they failed? She became frightened and dispirited, and pined for Ethyl's cool comfort.

2. REACHING OUT FOR HELP

Slowly it dawned on Hero that he must pocket his growing panic and pride and search for some help from experienced professionals. It had become unthinkable to imagine a single day without the glamorous duo over-seeing business from the Director's Office. Firing Ethyl and Morph was not going to be easy, because (and this was the simple truth) he had no one and no thing in mind to replace them. Nevertheless, he had heard mention of a personal business group that met weekly in the local church basement to discuss operating problems and solutions. He needed help and he needed answers. Perhaps he'd find some there.

It took several days to convince Hope to join him, but one Monday evening the Bests showered for (seemingly) hours, and Hope made up her face with unusual care. They trudged with pounding hearts down the steps to the meeting room, fervently hoping they wouldn't be forced to admit to their horrendous mistakes -- at least not all at once. They'd purposely left all the accounts and paperwork at home.

What the young, anxious couple discovered surprised them both. They were warmly greeted by several members, all of whom looked decidedly happy, and even content.

FIRST MEETING

"Hey! New-comers!" An older woman called out, running over to introduce herself. "Hi, I'm Faith. Grab some coffee and find a seat, because the meeting's about to start. I'll talk with you later." They poured themselves cups from a steaming urn and took seats at one of several tables set in a large circle.

Almost immediately, the leader knocked on the table top with his knuckles. "Welcome, everyone, to the regular Monday night open meeting of Benevolent Businesses. My name is Ernest, and I'm a Successful Businessman." The Bests were startled when everyone in the room called out cheerfully, "Hi, Ernest!"

Faith began to read out loud BB's Steps from a huge poster that hung on the wall behind Ernest.

TWELVE SUGGESTED STEPS OF
BENEVOLENT BUSINESSES

1. We admitted we were bankrupt.
2. Realized that an Advisory Committee could guide us in good business practices.
3. Made a decision to hire a new Boss to direct all aspects of the business.
4. Took thorough inventory of all departments.
5. Presented the Annual Report to the Boss and Advisory Committee.
6. Became ready to allow the Boss to re-design the product line.
7. Respectfully requested the Boss to take over daily operations.
8. Made a list of all customers who had received poor service or products and became willing to compensate them all.
9. Made direct payments and apologies to all customers, unless knowledge of illegal business practices would injure them or others.
10. Instituted strict quality control; immediately removed all defective items from production and notified and reimbursed customers fully.
11. Maintained daily communication with the Boss to enhance the process and quality of production, and to become motivated to follow through with all projects.
12. Having gained prosperity as a result of these steps, we shared our experience with other owners and observed these principles in all our business dealings.

"Look, Hero!" Hope sputtered in a sharp whisper. "Read number three!"

They made mental notes to ask questions after the meeting, as Ernest continued, "Tonight we'll be discussing the Third Step, which says, 'Made a decision to hire a new Boss to direct all aspects of the business.' I'll begin. My business was in terrible shape. No one would work for me; no one would speak to me. I'd lost two large office buildings and a factory. Corporate debt was in double-digit millions, and my common stock was scratched from the Big Board -- a true blow to my pride.

"I finally admitted to myself that Al Ego, my CEO and long-time buddy, was destroying the business. I needed you people to act as my Advisory Committee, and I had to put my absolute trust in the new Boss, whom I choose to call H.P. "I turned everything over to Him -- every record, invoice and key. Me, who never trusted anybody but EGO! I was so positive that Al and I together were an unbeatable team!"

The people seated at the tables chuckled appreciatively, as if they identified with Ernest. Hope noticed that the laughter was warm and genuine. No one seemed judgmental of this admission of corporate defeat.

Ernest looked at each face in turn, smiled with satisfaction and concluded, "I've never regretted the decision for a minute. Anyone else want to speak?"

And the discussion was simple and serious, as each businesswoman and man shared how hiring the right boss had transformed their businesses.

At last Hope could stand it no longer. "Please!" She protested, raising her hand. "How is it that everyone had trouble with an old CEO of the same name?" With that, the room broke into guffaws of laughter.

"It's not a family," Ernest explained, but a group known as the Executive Guidance Organization. They seem to sneak in and take charge whenever we're too lazy to do our own work."

After the meeting was over, several members of BB stayed to chat with the Bests, who asked many questions about hiring a new Boss. Someone handed Hope a simple business card of quality vellum stock. She found herself unconsciously stroking it with the tips of her fingers. The slightest wash of a rainbow glowed behind the engraved initials "H.P."

"Oh thanks,"she cried. "We'll call first thing tomorrow."

"No need to wait," Jake explained. "It's the decision the matters. H.P. has an 800 number and a twenty-four-hour hotline. Just make the first contact. And I'm glad to see you've already acted on the first two steps. Using that card means you're taking Step Three. Welcome to the club!"

3. DECISION TO HIRE

The Bests, over-stimulated by the coffee and conversation, couldn't fall asleep right away, but once Hero left a humble message on H.P.'s answering machine, a glorious feeling of relief and trust spread warmly through them both. Early the next morning, he followed up with a terse letter terminating the EGOs from employment (registered; return receipt requested) and was euphoric by the time he called Ernest. "We didn't sleep last night, but it's over. Nothing more to worry about. Mission accomplished!"

But Ernest slowly talked him down to reality, warning against over-confidence and simplistic thinking. "Nobody ever died from lack of sleep, old Buddy. And you've got to know that the tough time's just beginning. You've got a business to run."

Hero was incredulous. "We're hiring H.P. to do that. What are you talking about?"

"The Business of Life isn't quite that easy," Ernest explained patiently. "You'll be checking in with H.P. regularly, but the buggy-lugging is up to you. Start taking that Inventory, and don't forget to turn off your Paggles Switch. The EGOs always install one whenever they gain control of a Business."

Hero's pink cloud deflated instantly, but he hardly needed to explain that to Hope, who was feeling lost and depressed. Her closest friend Ethyl, her only true and constant companion, had just been torn from her, and she felt as if she needed to wear black crepe and a heavy veil. A phone call to Faith confirmed her feelings. "Of course you're depressed, Honey. You're going to be grieving for weeks. You're old life's gone, and it's okay to cry. Call me whenever you feel like it."

4. TAKING AN INVENTORY

The Best factory was largely mechanized, so it was able to run without direction for a few days. Hero and Hope didn't want to admit it to each other, but they were terrified to go near the place. They had ignored Life for so long that it was alien territory, and they knew they were over their depth. Courage was required, the kind of courage that the EGOs had always seemed to give them. Even daily phone calls to Ernest and Faith could only support them for so long, and a commitment to action was required. What was so frightening about a business inventory, after all? Couldn't they do it all when the employees were off on the weekend? Less embarrassing for everyone.

Saturday morning they psyched themselves up enough to unlock the heavy door that defended Life from outsiders, and the couple stepped across the threshold onto the factory floor with Trepidation, their skittish black mongrel dog. All the assembly lines were silent and still, but someone had left on the intercom. A popular negative rap was blaring:

"You ain't no good and you can't make it;
Get out now before you break it!"

"Wonderful stuff to work to -- great for morale!" Hero shouted scornfully into Hope's ear, forgetting that it was the very same message he'd heard incessantly from his own parents when he was young. He hunted desperately for a switch or volume control, but found neither.

The repetitious rap was maddening, but the factory itself disturbed them more. It was dirty and run down, as if no one had cared about it for years. A set of parallel assembly lines, labeled "Hero" and "Hope," ran the length of the huge building. Only a common roof represented their marriage, and the symbolism wasn't lost to either of them.

On Hero's side, a hundred cartons of Rage and Resentment were stacked on wooden skids by the bay door, ready for shipment. Along the wall rested bins of Arrogance tied with mylar balloons proclaiming "Number 1" in red letters. He picked one up, and discovered it was disturbingly light and insubstantial. When he shook it tentatively, beads of Macho and Selfishness rattled around inside. Hero was mortified.

Hope's produce was no less distressing. Stacks of carefully packaged Martyrdom and Intolerance were tightly strapped with wires of Sarcasm, while thousands of strips of Disapproval leaned against the wall, waiting to be counted and bundled. For many minutes, Hope simply hung her head, unable to look five feet in front of herself. Finally she picked up her pad and pencil and began half-heartedly to write down what she'd discovered, while the murderous Rap pounded in her ears.

Hero pulled himself together enough to run up the open iron stairs to the switchboard. Just as he's suspected, he was faced with two panels labeled "Hero" and "Hope." Paggles Switches dominated the center of each. They weren't actually switches at all, but large levers with shiny, black ball handles. Notches across the bottom of the lever system were stamped with the letters P-A-G-G-L-E-S; the notch up and to the left was marked ALL and to the right, OFF. What did the lever control? Hero gripped the cold metal ball tightly and forced it into the ALL position. After a long, hesitant moment the floor of the switchboard room vibrated, and a low rumble warned that gears had meshed and conveyor belts on the next floor were shifting into action.

He peered through the dim, dusty air toward his Assembly Line. Slowly at first, then with increasing rapidity, large cardboard cartons tumbled toward the catch-bin, stenciled in bold black letters, PRIDE, ANGER, GLUTTONY.... The young man guffawed when he realized that the other deadly sins, GREED, LUST, ENVY and SLOTH were sure to follow soon. Blackball indeed!

Hero slammed the lever into the OFF position and felt the gears and conveyors grinding slowly to a halt. At the same time, he noticed that the decibels of the Rap were cut by half.

"Honey!" He called down to Hope, who was wandering dazedly through the warehouse alleys. "Come on up! Turn off your Paggles Switch!" (He knew instinctively that she must turn it off herself.)

But Hope was past hearing. Trepidation, who had been snuffling out rodents around the dumpster, began to bark fiercely, and the distraught woman bolted for the back door by the loading bay.

"Shut up, Trep!" she snapped, as she dashed out to Ethyl's waiting car -- a huge sedan with glove-leather upholstery that Hope always thought of as the "Womb with a View." She opened the door, slid inside and slammed it shut in one continuous motion before Hero could reach the loading platform to shout "NO!"

He watched helplessly as the enormous car sped through the gate and careened around the corner out of sight. Several huge chunks of Reservation broke loose from the weakened factory ceiling and crashed onto Hope's conveyor belt, jamming the system.

A LESSON IN REALITY

Hero wanted no part of his old behavior, calling on Morph to make all the decisions. Instead, he phoned Ernest immediately, and reported what he had found at the factory, and how Hope had reacted with such vehemence.

After a long discussion, Ernest said, "I'd like to give you some homework, because our BB philosophy is filled with paradoxes that are nevertheless true. Think about this statement:

> We are powerless over everything,
> <u>and</u> responsible for everything."

"That's nonsense!" protested Hero.

"Just think about it over the weekend, and let me know what you come up with. See ya Monday night," Ernest replied cheerfully as he hung up the phone.

Hero spent the rest of the weekend working around the house, washing dishes, walking the dog, raking leaves and trying his damnedest to feel lighthearted, although Hope's disappearance gnawed at his gut. Half of him wanted to storm over to the EGOs and drag her home, but his more rational half knew that it would be pointless.

We make our own choices, he realized, and then we live by our decisions, no matter what we blame them on. Changing is tough. Ernest's paradox played in the back of his mind. It was strange that no one had ever thrown such an idea at him before. It was precisely the opposite of his parents' blame-riddled philosophy.

THOROUGH AND FEARLESS

Hero arrived at the meeting a full half-hour early, to find Ernest seated at a table, idly playing with his coffee cup. "I understand the paradox," he began. "I have no control over people, places and things, but I'm entirely accountable for my own attitudes and actions toward them. Damn it, Ernest, that's not the way I was brought up!" And the two of them laughed together in easy camaraderie. Hope, sneering, would have labeled it "male bonding."

The room slowly filled. Moments before the meeting began, Hope and Faith walked through the door together. Hope searched for her husband in the small crowd. She looked absolutely dreadful. Black circles rimmed her eyes; her blouse and hair were rumpled, and she wore no make-up. Nevertheless, something about the set of her shoulders and jaw signaled dignity and determination.

She walked over to Hero, and whispered in his ear, "Ethyl's no friend of mine." Her husband looked across at Faith, who nodded in agreement. Hero knew something fine was happening, and he had the good sense not to bombard the women with questions.

Art the Accountant, tonight's leader, knocked for attention. "Hi, everyone. My name is Art, and I'm a Successful Businessman. Hope and Hero called out, "Hi, Art," along with the other members. This was not like the previous week's gathering, because the Fourth Step requires concerted action and resolve.

Art read the Step, "Took thorough inventory of all departments," and then commented, "The Steps may be suggested, but I think of this Inventory as mandatory. We won't be able to change our production line if we don't know what we're producing right now. It's less painful than I thought it would be. For example, I used to ship out huge cartons of bitter Stinginess, but now I've re-tooled and manufacture small packets of a very attractive Thriftiness. (Laughter.) It has a lot to do with motivation, and avoiding EGO's influence."

Faith raised her hand. "I have to be sure my inventory is a balanced one, covering both the negatives and positives. It's awfully easy for me to beat myself up."

From the corner by the door came a hesitant voice. "What if you don't have any positive items at all on your assembly line?"

"Oh, come now," Faith replied sharply. "That's EGO talk, Virginia. If you can't be the best of the best, it sounds like you're willing to settle for the worst of the worst. Have you hired HP?"

Virginia nodded.

"Asking for direction every day?"

Virginia nodded again, with a little smile.

"I'll bet a large run of top-quality Willingness is rolling off your assembly line at this very moment!" Faith commented.

Several members voiced their agreement.

Virginia's smile broadened. "Thanks, Faith. I never thought of it that way."

Then Hope spoke up. "I have to admit I spent the weekend with Ethyl, because I thought she was a friend who'd never let me down. I learned an important lesson. The truth is that I've never wanted to be responsible for *anything* in my whole life. I wanted The Business to be hassle-free. Well, Life can't prosper that way, so I'm here to do what you and H.P. tell me to do." And she reached out for Hero's hand. It was a touching moment, and the group sat in silent respect for her honesty. Over at the Best's factory one last, tiny chunk of Reservation dropped to the floor and shattered. The automated robot-janitor, re-activated as soon as the EGOs left, whisked the shards out of sight into the dumpster. At the same time, a short, solid run of Surrender wrapped in broad sheets of Defeat began to slide quietly down her conveyor belt into the catch-bin.

That night, the Bests formally asked Ernest and Faith to be their Benevolent Business Mentors. Faith promised them an adventure, and so it was.

Guided by Ernest and Faith, the Bests' Inventories took several weeks. They uncovered piles of outdated merchandise in dark warehouse corners, and turned up dusty invoices and old bills of lading in their bottom desk drawers. The final tallies involved less pain than they originally anticipated, because of that first willingness to ask for help. The EGOs stopped by only once during a particularly hectic Holiday season, when the owners were pressured to produce perfect packages for every circumstance. The Bests were proud of the way they refused Ethyl and Morph admission to a Business affair.

Suddenly Self-esteem became the leader in their new product line. It was consumed entirely in-house.

ADJUSTING TO THE NEW BOSS

Hope and Hero worked steadily at the factory, and became increasingly skillful and self-responsible. They learned The Business from the mailroom up, always with the direction and support of their mentors. They attended BB meetings every week without fail, sometimes even traveling to Speaker Meetings in nearby towns.

The BB philosophy imparted a new zest to The Business of Life, which was showing signs of prosperity under the direction of H.P.

And that was the odd part. No one ever saw the new Boss, although evidence of His direction was everywhere. In fact, even the sex of the new Boss was open to speculation. Sometimes it seemed that they were dealing with a masculine presence, and at other times the circumstances strongly suggested a nurturing woman.

Employees offered a few observations of their own:

First, they came to believe that "Coincidences are H.P.'s way of remaining anonymous."

Then too, they discovered that "H.P. speaks through people."

Thirdly, many believed that H.P. often traveled about in disguise.

Surprisingly, these thoughts had a positive rather than a paranoid effect. In fact, employees at The Business became kinder and more concerned about everyone, friend and stranger alike. Morale rose, working conditions improved, productivity increased and quality control reached 99%. The plant was clean, freshly painted and cared for, and that awful rap music had been banned. Simply put, it was a pleasure to work at the Best Business.

5. PREPARING THE ANNUAL REPORT

Hero and Hope discovered that The Business had never published an Annual Report, because the EGOs had believed in spontaneity as the basis for operating the Business of Life. What nonsense! Most well run businesses have prioritized goals, and a series of one-year and five-year plans. When the Bests focused energy and attention on their Business, they realized that their marriage needed a comparable approach. They agreed to set aside the whole day of their anniversary each year to discuss dreams, goals, desires and financial plans. Instantly they felt more trusting and secure with each other, and wondered why more married couples didn't practice such a strategy.

Faith and Ernest recommended that this First Annual Business Report include all the sordid and satisfying details of the Inventory, and a complete Business History chronicling every major decision and production quota since the inception of the Business. When complete, it was a perfect-bound, slick-paper volume of over a hundred pages, with color glossies and impressive graphs. Several copies were presented to members of The Business's Advisory Committee (who were also members of their Monday night BB meeting) and a hardcover copy was left conspicuously on H.P.s desk.

Then Ernest and Hero headed for the mountains, where they spent a contented day hiking, fishing and discussing recurring themes and insights generated by this heavy report.

The women traveled to a small retreat house Faith owned at the shore for just this purpose. All four bowed their heads reverently for a moment before beginning, to acknowledge H.P's influence.

When the young couple returned home, it was clear that a profound cleansing had taken place in the presence of two caring friends.

6. ALLOWING H.P. TO DESIGN THE PRODUCT LINE

One Monday night, Ernest did most of the talking over dinner at the Diner before the regular meeting. Faith and the Bests listened intently, because Ernest had been practicing BB principles the longest, and presumably had some valuable experience to share. "Well, now," he was saying over his refill of coffee, "you two are ready to begin the tough part."

Hero reacted as if he'd been struck. "*Tough* part? What do you think it's been like up to now? Ernest, I swear you're astounding!"

"Hear me out," Ernest replied with a gentle smile. "Steps Six and Seven are the true core of the BB program. Too often, owners have to admit 'I can't give up this perc or power -- not yet.' But Step Six is talking about a systems-wide overhaul. Unless you understand that, your Business will merely improve a bit and then reach a production plateau."

"I don't get it," Hero protested. "You're telling me to give up *permanent* control of *my very own business!*"

Faith explained further. "Hero, several months ago you made a decision to hire a new CEO. This step verifies your willingness to maintain that relationship."

"For how long?" Hero asked, with a touch of panic in his voice. "Who knows better than <u>me</u> what I ought to manufacture?" At his factory, the heavy beat of the drop-forge, like a pounding fist, echoed through the plant. At that very instant, thickly insulated packages of Self-Will and Self-Reliance, still hot from the blast-furnace process, were being loaded by fork-lift and stacked at the front door where everyone -- employees and customers alike -- bumped into them on the way in or out.

His question hung suspended between them for a long moment. Then Hope reached over and laid her hand gently on top of his. "They're telling us that H.P. does." Her voice was low.

7. H.P. IN CHARGE OF DAILY OPERATIONS

Ernest nodded. "We're not saying that your whole business has been faulty. No indeed. But I remember that last year's inventory included a whole lot of Macho, Selfishness and Lust, all designed by the EGOs with your express approval. Are you willing to give up the manufacture of those products entirely? They've done a good deal of damage to your marriage. Can you accept H.P.'s new line of Serenity Gifts instead? The best sellers are Honesty, Acceptance, Tolerance and Unconditional Love."

Hero looked at the three of them in astonishment; slowly the light of understanding gleamed in his eyes. "Shift direction entirely? New priorities? New merchandise? All to H.P.'s taste, not mine? Whew! That's a tall order, but.... sure, I can do it!"

Hero looked relieved and relaxed, as if a burden had been lifted from his shoulders. And yet, on his Assembly Line, easily concealed parcels of personal-size Demands, Me's and My-Ways were being hurried into a side room of the warehouse for possible future use, and the stockroom ordered several cartons of Yabut screws in case the cutting machines needed repair.

Not knowing anything about these underground activities, Ernest was equally relieved. "Great! You need to stop by the factory tonight and write a memo announcing that you've officially asked H.P. to take over all aspects of daily operations. Remember, that doesn't mean you can sit back and relax."

Hope, who had been quiet through most of the dinner and discussion, spoke up with conviction, "I'm willing. I feel better just knowing I don't have to be right or perfect all the time. H.P. can ditch my run of Obsession immediately." Even as she spoke, any remaining desire to see Ethyl evaporated, and plain-wrapped, unmarked packets of Humility were rolled into the Warehouse Annex for use throughout the winter.

"I'm calling a Benefits Committee together next week," she went on, "because I don't need such a large percentage of the profits; the employees deserve a better Health and Holidays package, and I'd like a Child-care Center on the grounds. It would be good for all of us."

"Why are you *doing* all this?" Hero protested, thinking of the profits she'd be throwing away.

But it was apparent that Hope was firmly rejecting the business practices that the EGOs had taught her and revising her Employer-Employee Relations. Even as she spoke, the Art Department was pasting up a new two-page spread on Neighborliness, made up of equal parts Respect, Tolerance and Acceptance, for the mail order catalog, with a banner headline declaring "Fully guaranteed or double your money back." The text recommended ordering a small amount, because it was super-industrial strength.

"Mix a teaspoon into a quart of Quarrels and dissolve most Disagreements instantly."

8. MAKING A LIST OF ALL WRONGED CUSTOMERS

The Bests sometimes thought that their Mentors were pushing them rather hard and fast. It was barely a week later that the couple was asked to make a list of all customers who had ever been wronged by the Best Business, either by being sold defective products or by receiving poor or inconsiderate service.

"And that means every customer, no matter how long ago," Faith explained. "Remember when you were first practicing business skills, selling homemade lemonade to the neighbors? Did you cheat on the amount of lemons? Inflate the price? Forget to wash out the pitcher? These people go at the top of the list. You've done a thorough history for the Annual Report, so it won't be difficult."

Ernest stepped in here. "Many times, the people on your list will have mistreated you as well. Don't get caught up in self-righteousness. Focus on your own responsibility."

Hope and Hero were soon astonished by the size of their lists, which had involved several days of real soul-searching for them both. Again they noticed many recurring themes. They also considered the fact that, after Ethyl and Morph entered the picture, customer complaints increased and business associates were lost. Caught up as they were in the glamour of the fast lane, they'd never noticed how many acquaintances had walked out on them over the years -- shabbily treated by the Best Business.

Once the lists were complete, their Mentors asked them to go to a quiet place, read the names aloud slowly, with attention to each indiscretion, and then say out aloud, "I'm willing to compensate each and every one of you."

Hero balked at this. "Every one of them? I'll bet some of them are dead. We'll never be able to do it. You're crazy, Ernest!"

But Hero's Mentor maintained his equilibrium. "It's another step in cleaning up your past business practices, Hero. It's the willingness that counts."

Faith said, "There's just one other thing. Did you put yourselves at the top of the list of those you've hurt?" Both of them nodded emphatically. Hope explained, "For a while I thought I'd hurt only myself, but that soon changed when I got honest."

Now, at last, the Bests understood what damage they'd done to their Public Relations. It had been a powerful experience. Over at the plant, Remorse and Determination taped with wide strips of Willingness were stacking up rapidly in hundred-pound boxes on the rough wooden skids.

9. FULL PAYMENT AND APOLOGIES

The Bests had been comfortable regulars at the Monday Step Meeting for over four months. Tonight the subject was again the Ninth Step. Hope didn't remember a thing about the discussion twelve weeks ago, and she was determined to listen this time. Her List was complete. Some now had the word "(deceased)" after them. Others had three asterisks, "***", meaning *special attention.* The problem was daunting, overwhelming. Hope needed direction, and was willing to take it. She was pretty sure that Hero felt the same way.

Charlie the Car Dealer was running the meeting this night. The Ninth was his favorite Step, and he liked to be the leader whenever possible. "When I approach an associate who needs an apology, I'd first better check my attitude. It's a painful subject. Serious business. So I take my time, and discuss each circumstance with my Mentor before proceeding. It can be frightening. People may not respond as you would like them to -- and they don't <u>have</u> to, either!" (Laughter.)

Faith raised her hand. "I'd like to second your remark on taking plenty of time, Charlie, and yet not getting permanently sidetracked. For me, this Step has meant finally becoming responsible for my actions. I started to grow up at the age of forty three, I think."

Then Art the Accountant spoke. "Many of the people on my list were already dead, and at first I was relieved that I wouldn't have to face them. One was my own mother. I'd borrowed a lot of money from her under false pretenses when my buddy EGO was in charge of the store. I finally wrote her an honest, detailed letter, and then burned it, with a little prayerful ceremony. It helped to relieve some of my guilt. By the way, I'm going to be paying Step Nine debts for several more years, and it feels great!"

Hope looked across the table at her husband, and was surprised by narrowed eyes and a closed expression. Something wasn't quite right, she thought, but it was only the faintest gut reaction. Then his face cleared and he smiled at her.

Perhaps she'd been mistaken.

10. STAYING ON TOP OF QUALITY CONTROL

"'Good products make for repeat business,'" Ernest was sharing slogans as he and Hero sat over a cup of coffee in Hero's kitchen. Or try these: 'The Customer is always right,' and 'Service with a smile.' He paused. What's the matter, Hero?"

"I guess I'm just frustrated," Hero answered through clenched teeth. "For one thing, H.P. has never showed His face in my office. In fact, I'm hearing rumors that **no** one's ever seen Him. What did I get myself into, anyway? And, I'm sick to death of being told what to do. My Business is going damned well, thank you, and I'm pretty proud of my accomplishments."

"Usually when an owner decides to take control again, it's by using the unethical business practices that EGO taught him. Please remember that the Tenth Step has three parts to it. First, daily inventory allows for consistent quality control. Second, it reminds you to make immediate apologies and compensate a customer whenever defective merchandise somehow slips through to the retail market. -- and every so often it will. We strive for progress, not perfection.

"The third part isn't written, but it's clearly implied. A daily inventory will warn you immediately if the Paggles Switch has been reactivated, so that you can make adjustments to the Attitude Regulator. From the way you're talking, I can tell you that a load of Resentment has been piling up on your loading dock."

"There's nothing more you can teach me, Ernest. I'll thank you to leave my house right now!" Hero's meaning was unmistakable. He flung the door open and glared angrily at his Mentor with undisguised distaste.

Hope was just coming up the walk to her house.

"Well, now you know what's been happening," she said, noticing Ernest's expression of distress. "I wish there were something I could do. He's been like that for several days now."

"Yes, there <u>is</u> something," Ernest replied with unusual intensity. "Pay attention to your <u>own</u> merchandise, and practice Step Ten with him as if he were just another customer. See ya Monday night. It's my favorite. The Eleventh Step."

11. LEARNING HOW TO COMMUNICATE WITH THE BOSS

Hope came to the BB meeting alone. Hero had disappeared for several days, and she had no intention of heading out to find him. Although she was saddened by her husband's decision, Hope was firmly focused on her own Business, and trusted the BB principles to carry her through. It was no accident, she was thinking, that her Mentor's name was Faith.

BB meetings always start on time, because it is responsible behavior and good practice for all business dealings. A BB slogan says it this way: "Promptness is a promise kept."

So Faith rapped for attention exactly at the hour, and introduced herself as a "Grateful Businesswoman, thanks to H.P. and all of you."

"Hi, Faith," the group called out to her with unusual enthusiasm. Faith was especially well loved by the group, Hope realized, because she lived the BB Program to the best of her ability -- and it showed in all her business affairs.

"The Eleventh Step is difficult for new members to understand," she began, "because it talks about communicating daily with H.P., but we all know how hard it is to catch Him at His desk! (Appreciative laughter.)

I've been to training sessions that teach communication techniques with bosses. It seems that many CEOs like to be contacted only through memos; others expect thick documents full of charts and graphs. Some like early-morning discussions over breakfast; others expect to get their hands dirty on the factory floor. A few only want information to be filtered through their VPs; others expect to meet each employee as the need arises. And heaven help the worker who uses a technique different from the one his boss prefers!

"All good communication comes in four parts -- talking, listening, honesty and action. And that's what H.P. expects from me: to talk honestly awhile and share my needs, listen for the answers, and then take action. BB likes to call it Good Orderly Direction. If I sit quietly in my office and talk or write out my thoughts, H.P. will know about it, like a loving mother who responds to her child's feelings and needs before they've obvious to anyone else."

Hope suddenly glanced toward the back of the room. Hero was leaning against the doorjamb, arms folded tight across his chest, a derisive expression on his handsome face. Hope caught his eye for a second, but he quickly shifted his gaze away from hers.

Ernest continued the thought: "So I can't just sit back and do nothing, and I can't take over again whenever I feel like it, either. I believe that H.P. helps Businesses that help themselves. With daily communication, it gets easier to know what H.P. wants me to do. It's best for me to check with other BB members and my Mentor, of course, to be sure my thinking hasn't reverted to EGO practices."

Hope said, "I've noticed that Good Orderly Direction feels *right and peaceful*. In fact, it's usually not at the expense of other businesses, but actually helps other businesses at the same time. I believe that's just good business."

Several members of the group nodded in agreement. Hope turned toward her husband, but only caught a glimpse of his back as he turned away and hurriedly left the room.

DINER MEETING

Later, several members headed for the Diner, -- where, sometimes, the most important ideas are shared. The conversation turned to Hero's rejection of the BB Program.

Faith said, "He knows what to do. I hope he contacts H.P. soon."

Art commented that an invisible Higher Power or CEO is often too much for newcomers at first. "I like to think of the Group together as a power greater than myself alone. An Advisory Committee's good enough at first, and if H.P. speaks through people, why, there you are."

"I'm sorry my husband didn't hear you say that," Hope said. "I know he's been having trouble giving up control, but the power of a group just might make sense to him."

12. LIVING THESE PRINCIPLES IN ALL OUR BUSINESS DEALINGS

In the first decade of the twentieth-first century, this organization of Benevolent Businesses has continued to flourish. Active chapters now exist in most countries around the world, and their corporate systems manual, titled Benevolent Businesses (a rather Big Book), is published in many languages. The organization has transformed the lives of millions.

Hope's personal enterprise has prospered over the past few years, just as Faith predicted it would, and the two of them have become close friends.

She seldom ever thinks about Ethyl, except at meetings, when the subject comes up. Hero has dropped by a couple of times, looking bleary-eyed and not quite healthy. They're still married, but in name only, and separating their two businesses was easier than Hope could have imagined. An electrical crew simply pulled in one day and removed Hero's control panel; No one was surprised that the Paggles Switch was jammed in the "ALL" position. Later, it was rumored that he'd also become hooked on Negative Rap.

Afterwards, Hope took over both sides of the factory, and reinstated the old airbrushed cherry-bowl trademark. Her catalog business has expanded rapidly. Neighborliness has sold so well that she's expanded into personal-size boutique packages of Tolerance and Acceptance tied with gold ribbons of Positive Regard. She's even now trying out a limited edition of Unconditional Love. It's heady stuff.

Hope has made Benevolent Businesses a way of life. She puts a good deal of energy into helping new-comers, and lives the Twelve Suggested Steps to the best of her ability. But she's hardly perfect. Even with a careful Daily Inventory, chips of Envy and Unrest show up in the styro-foam packing at times, along with Frustration. And she'll readily admit to believing -- sometimes several times a day -- that a few of her ideas might be better than H.P.'s.

HOPE'S MEETING

The Twelfth Step is her favorite. In fact, she led the meeting on that topic a couple of weeks back. Before rapping for attention, she searched the faces in the room, wondering who might be H.P. in disguise, (although she tends to believe that a bit of H.P's character is in everyone.)

"Hi, Everybody," she said with a smile. "My name is Hope. I'm a Successful Businesswoman -- and a Miracle. Following the spirit of the Twelfth Step, I've become a Mentor to several young women who keep my memory very green indeed! I've learned many important lessons in my years in BB, but the most important is this: in order to keep what I've learned, I must give it away. It's one of many delightful paradoxes. Isn't that right, Ernest?"

"Now, who would like to be the first to share their experience, strength and hope?"

ENGRAVED HALLMARK: *PROMISES*

At that moment, in the factories of just about every member sitting around the table that night, silver vials of Serenity wrapped in mauve silk velvet were gently lifted from the hand-finishing benches and presented as gifts to all the employees. The recipe is a secret of H.P.'s, and the catalyst is a pinch per pint each of Willingness, Acceptance, Trust and Joy.

The Serenity manufactured in these Benevolent Businesses is never put on the wholesale market, because it has a very short shelf-life and must be created fresh each and every day.

* * *

THE AUTHOR

... calls herself a Grateful Recovering Alcoholic. She was born in 1935, the same year as AA. Her Sobriety Date is May, 1970.

A native of New Jersey, she worked in the Addictions field for 21 years, moving to the Coast of Maine when she retired in 1996. She continues to be active in her 12 Step Group, and says that the Program continues to thrill her.

* * *

The Twelve Steps
of Alcoholics Anonymous*

1. We admitted we were powerless over alcohol -- that our lives had become unmanageable.

2. Came to believe that a Power greater than ourselves could restore us to sanity.

3. Made decision to turn our will and our lives over to the care of God as we understood Him.

4. Made a searching and fearless moral inventory of ourselves

5. Admitted to God, ourselves, and to another human being, the exact nature of our wrongs.

6. Were entire ready to have God remove all these defects of character.

7. Humbly asked Him to remove our shortcomings.

8. Made a list of all persons we had harmed, and became willing to make amends to them all.

9. Made direct amends to such people wherever possible, except when to do so would injure them or others.

10. Continued to take personal inventory and when we were wrong promptly admitted it.

11. Sought through prayer and meditation to improve our conscious contact with God as we understood Him, praying only for knowledge of His will for us and the power to carry that out.

12. Having had a spiritual awakening as the result of these steps, we tried to carry this message to alcoholics, and to practice these principles in all our affairs.

* * *